The History and Activities of

# NATIVE
# AMERICANS

## Lisa Klobuchar

Heinemann Library
Chicago, Illinois

© 2006  Heinemann Library,
a division of Reed Elsevier, Inc.
Chicago, Illinois

Customer Service  888-454-2279
Visit our website at www.heinemannraintree.com

Designed by Richard Parker and Tinstar Design Ltd (www.tinstar.co.uk)
Printed and bound in China by WKT Company Limited

10 09 08 07 06
10 9 8 7 6 5 4 3 2 1

Library of Congress Cataloging-in-Publication Data

Klobuchar, Lisa.
  The history and activities of Native Americans / Lisa Klobuchar.
      p. cm. --  (Hands-on American history)
  Includes bibliographical references and index.
  ISBN 1-4034-6054-X -- ISBN 1-4034-6061-2 (pbk.)
  1. Indians of North America--History. 2. Indians of North
America--Material culture. 3. Indian craft--North America. I. Title. II.
Series.
  E77.4.K57 2005
  973.04'97--dc22
                            2004003882

**Acknowledgments**
The author and publishers are grateful to the following for permission to reproduce copyright material: Corbis pp. 13 (Jan Butchofsky-Houser), 12 (Robert van der Hilst), 8, 9, 16; Getty Images p. 24 (The Image Bank); Harcourt Education pp. 19, 23, 27, 29 (Janet Moran); Minnesota Historical Society p. 7; Peter Newark's American Pictures pp. 10, 14, 15, 18; Werner Forman Archive pp. 6, 11, 17, 20.

Cover photographs by Werner Forman Archive and Peter Newark's American Pictures

# Contents

Some words are shown in bold, **like this**. You can find out what they mean by looking in the glossary.

# Chapter 1: America's First People

Native Americans were the first people to settle in North and South America. Many cultural historians and anthropologists believe that they arrived from Asia between 15,000 and 35,000 years ago. They may have walked across a land bridge that once connected the eastern part of what is now Russia to what is now Alaska. They were probably following herds of large animals that they hunted. These original Americans eventually lived everywhere from the cold northern regions all the way to the southern tip of South America.

This map shows the locations of the different 19th century Native American tribes.

## TIME LINE

| 33,000–13,000 B.C.E | 7,000 B.C.E. | 2,000 B.C.E. | 1492 C.E. | 1607 |
|---|---|---|---|---|
| Native Americans arrive in North America from Asia. | Native Americans begin to farm. | Native Americans set up first permanent villages. | Christopher Columbus lands in North America and gives the people there the name Indians. | First English settlement in America founded in Jamestown, Virginia; settlers and Native Americans have generally friendly relationship. |

These people formed different tribes, or nations, and developed their own unique **cultures**. People who study human culture have arranged Native American tribes into culture groups. All the tribes within these culture groups share similar beliefs, **traditions**, and ways of life. In the United States and Canada, there are ten culture groups. These include the Arctic, Subarctic, Northeast, Southeast, Plains, the Northwest Coast, California, the Great Basin, Plateau, and Southwest.

The way of life of Native Americans depended on the climate and land where they lived. In the Northeast and Southeast, rich soil, plenty of rain, and a pleasant climate allowed the Native Americans to live in permanent villages and develop a culture based on farming. Farming was much harder in the dry desert conditions of the Great Basin and Plateau. These Native Americans got their food by hunting and gathering. Because the Plains groups depended on the buffalo for much of their livelihood, they developed a **nomadic** lifestyle. They moved constantly, following buffalo herds across the prairie.

| 1830 | 1840s–1900 | 1876 | 1924 |
|---|---|---|---|
| Indian Removal Act forces eastern tribes to move west of the Mississippi to make room for settlers. | U.S. government gradually forces almost all Native Americans to move to **reservations**. | Battle of Little Big Horn. | Indian Citizenship Act gives citizenship to all Native Americans born in the United States. |

## On the move

A common image of the Native Americans of the Plains region is of a mighty warrior or hunter on horseback, galloping into battle or chasing buffalo. But for most of Native American history, the horse was completely unknown. Native Americans did all their traveling on foot or by boat. Some groups used dogs to pull flat sleds called travois. But long-distance traveling was difficult, if not impossible.

A great change came when Spanish settlers first brought horses from Europe in the 1500s. The lifestyles of the Plains

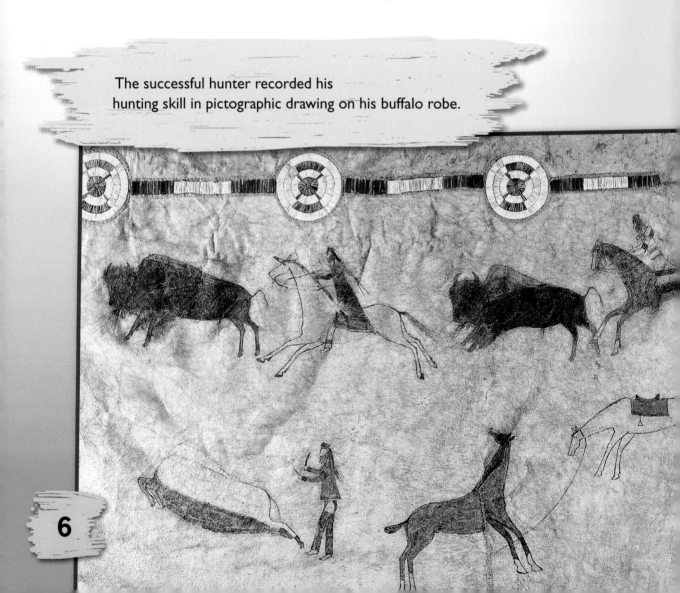

The successful hunter recorded his hunting skill in pictographic drawing on his buffalo robe.

groups, including the Dakota and the Mandan, changed. With horses, Native Americans could travel faster and carry heavier loads. Cone-shaped buffalo-skin tents called tepees replaced permanent homes in villages. Entire villages could travel long distances to follow herds of buffalo. Gradually, hunting became their main source of food, rather than farming. They gave up their settled way of life and became **nomads**.

Many of the objects made and used by the Plains and Plateau Native Americans were designed to fit in with their nomadic way of life. Tepees could be put up or taken down quickly and carried easily. Mothers strapped their infants into cradleboards, which were animal-skin bags on a wooden frame. This made it easy for mothers to carry babies on their backs.

## NATIVE AMERICANS OR AMERICAN INDIANS?

Some historians refer to the native peoples of North America as Indians, as Christopher Columbus did, or Amerinds. Some people prefer the term American Indians. Others call them Native Americans, as this book does. The native people of Canada are usually called First Nations People.

This woman is using a cradleboard to carry her small child.

## Settlers and Native Americans

Europeans began arriving in the United States in large numbers in the 1500s. Their relationships with Native Americans varied from region to region and culture to culture.

A group called the Hopi tried to befriend settlers from Spain when they came into contact. The settlers attempted to convert the Hopi to Christianity and in some cases forced the Hopi to work for them. In 1680 the Hopi and other Native Americans revolted against the treatment they were receiving from the Spaniards.

In the 1800s, settlers began moving west. By the 1870s, they had killed off most of the buffalo the Plains tribes depended on for their survival. The Plains tribes fought for their way of life. In 1868 the U.S. government signed a treaty with the Sioux chief, Red Cloud. This treaty gave the Sioux the land now known as North and South Dakota as a **reservation**.

Chief Red Cloud had a vision about the battle of Little Big Horn.

A memorial to those killed in the massacre at Wounded Knee.

However, in 1874 gold was found in South Dakota. The U.S. army tried to remove the Native Americans from the area so that settlers would be able to dig for gold. The Cheyenne, Sioux, and Arapaho united against the army. In 1876 the Native Americans won a victory at the Battle of Little Big Horn.

This victory led to more U.S. soldiers entering the area. In 1889 the Sioux reservation was split into six smaller ones. In December a group of unarmed Sioux were killed at Wounded Knee. The Plains tribes did not go to war again.

The Plateau tribes had a similar experience when settlers began pouring into the Oregon Territory. The U.S. government arranged for the Native American groups to live on reservations. In 1860 gold was found on the Nez Perce reservation. The U.S. wanted to move the Nez Perce to a new location. A war broke out between the Nez Perce and the United States. The war lasted until 1877.

Native American life varied greatly across the country. What groups wore, ate, and where they lived all depended on their **culture** and the climate where they lived. Some elements were similar from place to place.

## Bowls from the earth

Native American groups throughout North America made and used pottery vessels for cooking and storage. Pottery vessels were very good for these purposes, but not all groups used them. For the **nomadic** tribes of the Plains and Plateau, pottery was too bulky and heavy to carry from place to place.

Pottery making was traditionally the job of women. The best pottery makers belonged to Native American culture groups that lived in permanent villages, such as those in the Southeast and Southwest. The Native Americans of the

This 1905 photo shows a Hopi woman making pots.

Totem poles were usually erected at potlaches and formed the link between the natural phenomena and humans.

Southwest, such as the Hopi and the Zuni, were, and still are, known for their beautiful pottery. Hopi women are also known for making beautiful baskets and blankets.

## Important objects

Native Americans made many objects that were both **symbols** and useful tools, such as shields and weapons for hunting. Warriors sometimes carried a small version of their shield. They believed this mini shield would protect them in battle. Native Americans of the Pacific Northwest made totem poles to show wealth, power, and family history. Southwest Native Americans believed in friendly spirits called Kachinas. Zunis and Hopis made Kachina dolls to symbolize the spirits, and to teach their children.

Many Native American groups used peace pipes to show friendship. Before important meetings they would blow smoke from the pipe in all directions.

## Children

In most tribes, children did not attend school the way we do today. Instead, children were taught the skills and history they needed to know by their parents and other adults.

Among many groups, such as the Sioux and the Hopi, children were named for things in nature. For example, a child might be given the name Lone Bull or Running Water.

By the age of five, Sioux children could swim and ride horses. They also learned how to hunt with bows and arrows. Girls made dolls and miniature tepees. These were not just toys. They helped the girls learn skills they would need later in life. Boys had races and played other games that helped them learn skills they would need as warriors. By the age of seventeen, boys were ready to become warriors.

These modern Lakota Sioux children are dressed for a Pow Wow.

Many of the games Hopi children played were thought to help nature. The Hopi believed that playing with tops helped the wind to blow and a form of kickball helped the water fill the streams.

Most groups held coming of age ceremonies. Among the Plateau tribes, girls lived alone for months at a time and took sweat baths to help them become strong. They hoped to get a guardian spirit to protect them throughout their lives. Among the Sioux, an older woman stayed with the girl. Boys found their guardian spirits by going on vision quests. A boy would travel to an isolated spot. The boy would stay there alone without food, water, or weapons. The guardian spirit might appear to him in the form of an animal.

The inside of a modern sweat lodge.

13

Many Native American groups loved games and sports. Running races and wrestling matches were popular throughout North America as were breath holding, laughing, and jumping contests. Many Native American groups also played guessing games.

Many games were played in slightly different forms throughout North America. Southeastern Native American groups played a game called chungke, or chunkey, on a rectangular court. Two players used long poles to nudge a stone disk on its side. Other players threw their sticks at the disk. Whoever's stick landed closest to where

## LACROSSE

Lacrosse is probably the most famous Native American game. Players used sticks with pouches on their ends to toss and throw a hard ball to one another. Points were scored by passing the ball through goalposts. Teams could be made up of 100 or more players, and the playing field might be a mile (1.6 kilometers) long.

Native Americans of the Great Lakes of Canada playing a game.

the disk stopped rolling earned points. Among the Plains tribes, a similar game was called hoop-and-pole. Players rolled a netted hoop along while other players tried to spear it.

In a popular women's game called shinny, players used a curved stick to knock a ball through the other team's goal markers. Women also played double ball, in which they used sticks to throw and catch two balls connected by **rawhide**. The object of the game was to get the double ball through the other team's goal markers.

Children played with dolls, tops, rattles, balls, carved animal figures, and whistles made of bone or pottery. Other toys were smaller versions of adult tools. Boys had small bows and arrows, slingshots, and knives. Girls had dishes, baskets, pots and pans, and other supplies used by women.

Kachina dolls look like toys, but are actually important religious items.

## Music and dance

Music played a role in every part of Native American life. Native Americans held ceremonies and celebrations throughout the year, and music and dance were always a part of them. Native Americans played music during ceremonies to heal sick people, and they also enjoyed it along with dancing.

Jemez Indians performing the green corn dance.

A "love flute" used during courtship.

The three main instruments used in Native American music were the drum, the rattle, and the wooden flute. Drums were used to keep the rhythm during dances. There were two kinds of drums. Drums that had two heads could be played on both sides. Tom-toms had only one head. Drums and tom-toms were usually played by striking them with drumsticks. The body of a water drum was partially filled with water, which gave the drum a special sound. Some drums were so large that several drummers could play them at the same time.

All Native American tribes used rattles. They made them in different shapes and sizes and out of many kinds of materials, including gourds, wood, **rawhide**, pottery, and even turtle shells. They shook rattles with handles and also attached small rattles to their bodies to make noise as they danced.

Flutes are not as widespread in Native American music as drums and rattles, but they have been around for a long time. Flutes dating back 2,000 years have been found in North America. Among most tribes, only men played flutes. Native American flutes were not played sideways, as are modern flutes. They were played downward, like a modern clarinet or oboe.

# Chapter 4: Hands-on History

## WARNING!

**Always make sure an adult is present when using a hot stove.**

**Make sure to read all the directions before starting the recipe.**

This chapter will introduce you to aspects of life among some of the Native American culture groups. By doing the hands-on activities and crafts, you'll get a feel for the rich cultural **traditions** of North America's native people.

## Recipe: Make Wild Rice Pancakes

Most Native Americans did not have chicken eggs, wheat flour, baking powder, or milk in the 1800s. Native Americans living in the areas that are now Wisconsin and Minnesota harvested wild rice by canoe. Northern Native Americans collected sap from maple trees and boiled it into a sweet syrup.

This recipe gives you a chance to sample two popular traditional Northern Native American foods. Together they make a delicious breakfast treat.

Native Americans of Wisconsin harvesting wild rice.

1. Put the wild rice and water in a covered saucepan. Bring to a boil, then turn down heat to low. Simmer, covered, for an hour or until the rice grains break open. Remove from heat, uncover, and set aside to cool.

2. Measure the flour and baking powder into the mixing bowl. Gradually whisk in the milk. Whisk in the egg and beat until the batter is smooth.

3. Stir 1 cup of the cooked rice into the batter.

4. Heat the frying pan or griddle over medium heat. Add butter.

5. Spoon the batter into the hot frying pan or griddle by large spoonfuls.

6. Cook the pancake 3 to 5 minutes on each side until the pancakes are golden brown.

7. Serve with syrup if desired.

This recipe makes about seven pancakes.

## INGREDIENTS AND SUPPLIES

- 1/2 cup raw wild rice (available at most grocery stores)
- 1 1/4 cup water
- 1/4 cup flour
- 1 teaspoon baking powder
- 1/2 cup milk
- 1 egg
- 1 tablespoon butter
- maple syrup
- mixing bowl
- whisk
- nonstick frying pan or griddle saucepan with lid
- large spoon or ladle
- wide spatula

## Craft: Make a Parfleche

Native Americans of the Plateau and Plains moved around a lot. A parfleche was a **rawhide** carrying case with a patterned design. The pouch was made waterproof by using glue. Here you will use other materials to make a simple parfleche.

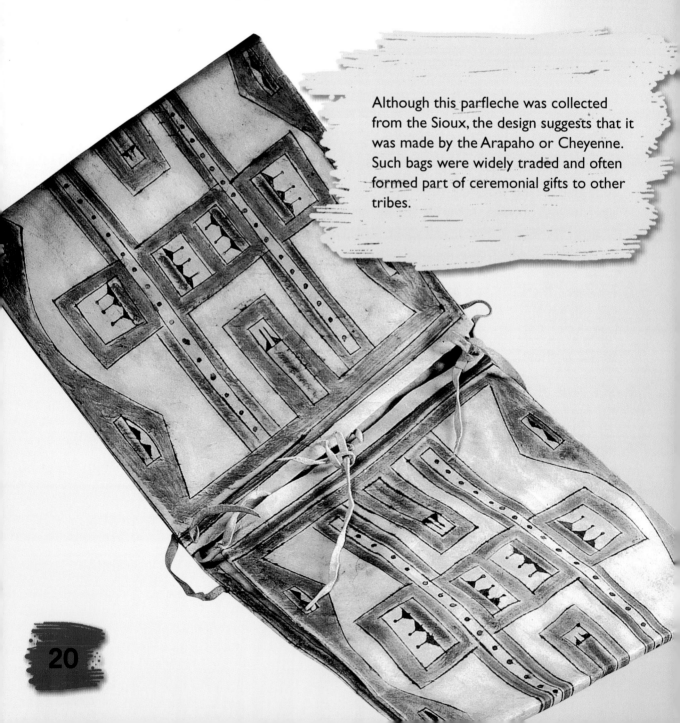

Although this parfleche was collected from the Sioux, the design suggests that it was made by the Arapaho or Cheyenne. Such bags were widely traded and often formed part of ceremonial gifts to other tribes.

## SUPPLIES

- tan or other light colored felt, vinyl imitation leather, or thin rawhide
- ruler
- scissors
- one-hole punch
- black permanent marker
- paint and paintbrushes
- yarn or leather cord

1. Cut a piece of felt 12 by 16 inches (30 by 40 centimeters). Cut the corners off to make rounded edges as shown. (See Picture A)

2. Punch four holes at the rounded ends of the cloth. (See Picture B)

3. Create a design for your parfleche on paper. *Will your design be original or copied from something else? What designs might a Native American have chosen?*

4. Use the black marker to draw your design onto the felt.

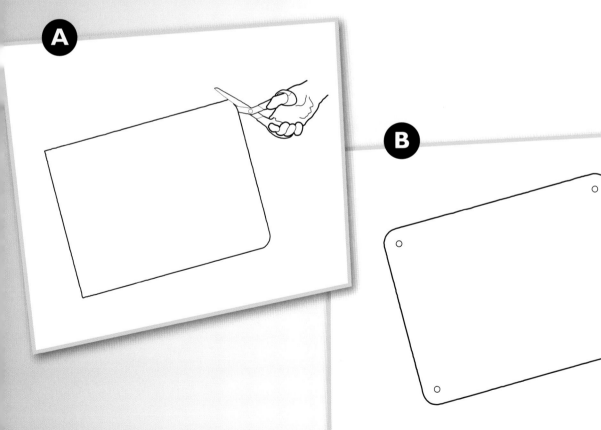

A

B

5. Use the paint to decorate your design.

6. When the paint is dry, fold the parfleche. Fold the long sides in about 2 inches (5 centimeters). This will make a rectangle. Then fold the ends in about 2 inches as well. (See Picture C)

7. Cut a piece of yarn, or leather cord, 8 inches (20 centimeters) long. Thread the piece through the holes to fasten the parfleche. (See Picture D)

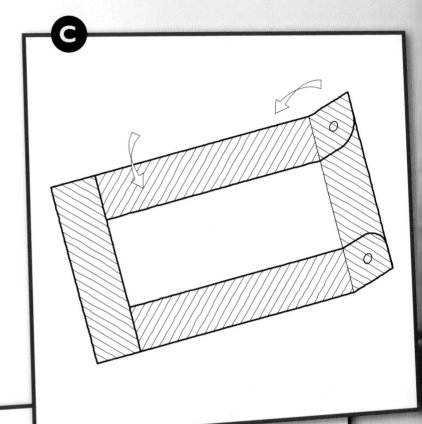

8. You may wish to punch more holes in other places on the parfleche. Having more holes will allow you to make the parfleche more secure. Holes should be created in pairs so that you can thread the yarn or cord through.

## Craft: Make a Dream Catcher

The Ojibwe of Wisconsin were the first Native American group to use dream catchers. They hung dream catchers over their babies' cradleboards to entertain the baby and ensure sweet dreams.

Dream catchers flying in Monument Valley.

**WARNING!**

Make sure to read all the directions before starting the project.

1. Cover the hoop by winding yarn or brown tape around it. Glue the yarn to the hoop at both ends.

2. Use leather cord or string to form the net-like strings in the center of your dream catcher. Use the same stitch from start to finish. To start, hold the string and place it loosely over the top of the hoop. Move the string around to the back of the hoop (forming a hole) and pull the string through the hole you just made. (See Picture A.)

## A NOTE ON SUPPLIES

Authentic hoops can be made from bent willow sticks tied with string or taped. Hoops should be about 6 inches (15 centimeters) across. Metal hoops can be bought at a craft store. Plastic hoops can be made by cutting the rim off a large plastic container. Hoops can also be made by bending coat hangers and taping down the ends, or by doubling up extra-long pipe cleaners.

## SUPPLIES

- hoop
- leather cord or string
- brown electrical tape or yarn
- small objects such as beads, feathers, shells
- glue

**A**

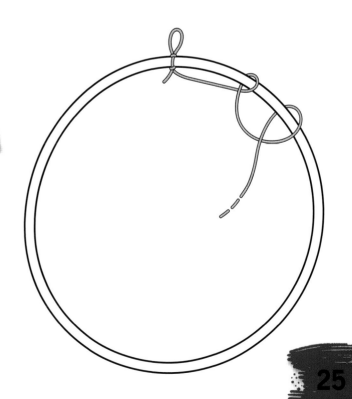

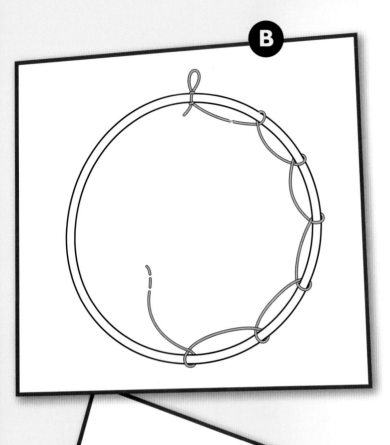

3. Continue around the hoop in this way, space the stitches evenly about 1 1/2-2 inches (4-5 centimeters) apart. Pull each stitch tight, but not too tight. If you pull the string too tight, it will warp the hoop. (See Picture B.)

4. When you reach the place where you started, you are ready to make the next inner circle of the net. Loop the cord between the previous stitches as shown. (See Picture C.) Continue in this way until only a small hole remains in the center. (See Picture D.)

5. When only a small hole remains in the center, tie a knot in the center, dab it with glue and cut off the extra cord or string.

6. Thread beads and other decorations onto some yarn, leather cord, or string. (See Picture E.) *How will you decide what objects to include?*

7. Tie and glue the strings to the sides and bottom of the dream catcher.

8. Make a hanger by tying or gluing a cord to the top of the dream catcher.

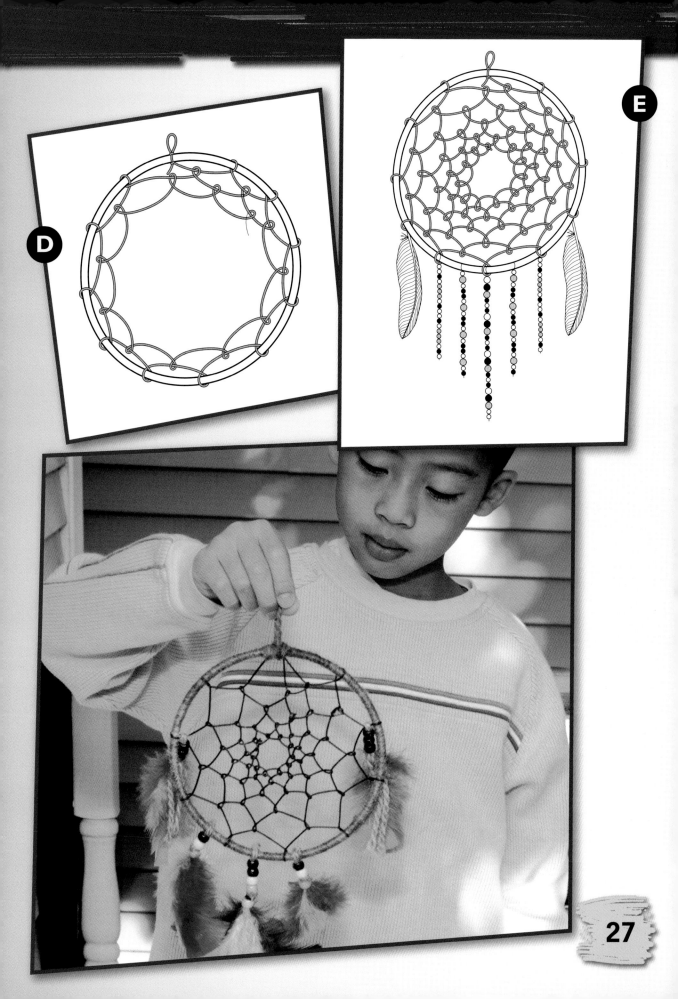

D

E

## Craft: Make a Ring and Pin Toy

Ring and pin toys were once popular throughout North America. The object of the game was to use a pin or stick to catch a target with holes in it. The target was often made of some kind of animal skin.

1. Peel the backing off of the contact paper. Place a sheet of paper along one edge, covering half of the sticky side of the contact paper. Now fold the contact paper over, sandwiching the sheet of paper inside. (See Picture A)

2. Take the contact paper you have folded and trim it into an oval or circle.

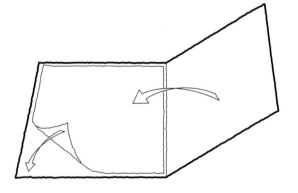

### SUPPLIES

- brown or tan contact paper, 14 by 7 inches (18 by 36 centimeters)
- sheet of white paper 7 by 7 inches (18 by 18 centimeters)
- white glue or hot glue
- scissors
- black permanent marker
- thin metal skewer or knitting needle, about 6 inches (15 centimeters) long
- 3 feet (1 meter) of leather or vinyl cord or twine
- 5 empty wooden thread spools
- 4 pony beads or small plastic beads
- brown and black paint (Permanent acrylic paint will adhere best to contact paper.)

*Note: Vinyl can be used instead of contact paper, but two sheets will need to be sandwiched together and glued.*

3. Draw circles on the contact paper as shown. Make one circle in the center bigger than the others. Cut out the circles. (See picture B)

4. Use a permanent black marker or paint around the edges of the holes and of the large circle with the black paint.

5. Wrap the leather cord around the hooked end of the skewer or knitting needle and glue it in place. Glue a bead to the end of the cord.

6. Paint the wooden spools. Decorate them by painting them brown and drawing or painting circles on them, if you want. *What other colors or designs could you add?*

7. Thread the spools onto the leather cord. String three beads onto the end of the loose end of the cord. Loop the cord through one of the holes close to the edge of the vinyl circle. Run the end of the cord back through the three beads and tie a knot.

Test the toy to find the right length for the cord to make the target easy to swing. Glue the end of the cord inside the three beads. When the glue is dry, trim off any extra cord.

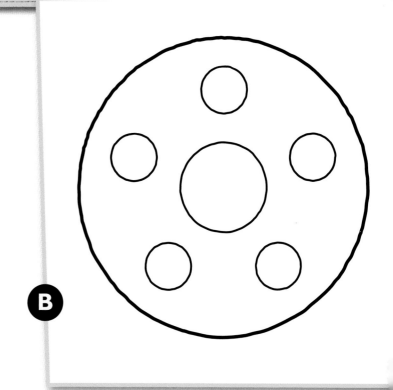

**B**

**culture** way of life of a group of people, including its beliefs, arts, and customs

**nomad** person who does not live permanently in one place. The word *nomadic* describes this way of life.

**rawhide** animal skin that has had all hair removed but has not been tanned into leather

**reservation** land set aside for a specific use

**symbol** something that stands for something else

**tradition** belief or practice that is passed down from one generation to another

## More Books to Read

Isaacs, Sally Senzell. *Life in a Hopi Village*. Chicago: Heinemann, 2002.

Isaacs, Sally Senzell. *Life in a Sioux Village*. Chicago: Heinemann, 2002.

You may also be interested in a series called Native Americans, published by Heinemann in 2003. This series has books on sixteen different Native American groups.

# A Note to Teachers

The instructions for these projects are designed to allow students to work as independently as possible. However, it is always a good idea to make a prototype before assigning any project, so that students can see how their own work will look when completed. Prior to introducing these projects, teachers should collect and prepare the materials and be ready for any modifications that may be necessary. Participating in the project-making process will help teachers understand the directions and be ready to assist students with difficult steps. Teachers might also choose to adapt or modify the lessons to better suit the needs of an individual student or class. No one knows what levels of achievement students will reach better than their teacher.

While it is preferable for students to work as independently as possible, there is some flexibility in regards to project materials and tools. They can vary according to what is available. For instance, while standard white glue may be most familiar to students, there might be times when a teacher will choose to speed up a project by using a hot glue gun to fasten materials for students. Likewise, while a project may call for leather cord, it is feasible in most instances to substitute vinyl cord or even yarn or rope. Acrylic paint may be recommended because it adheres better to a material like felt or plastic, but other types of paint would be useable as well. Circles can be drawn with a compass, or simply by tracing a cup, roll of tape, or other circular object. Obviously, allowing students a broad spectrum of creativity and opportunities to problem-solve within the parameters of a given project will encourage their critical thinking skills most fully.

Each project contains an italicized question somewhere in the directions. These questions are meant to be thought-provoking and promote discussion while students work on the project.

# Index